The NATURE of Matter

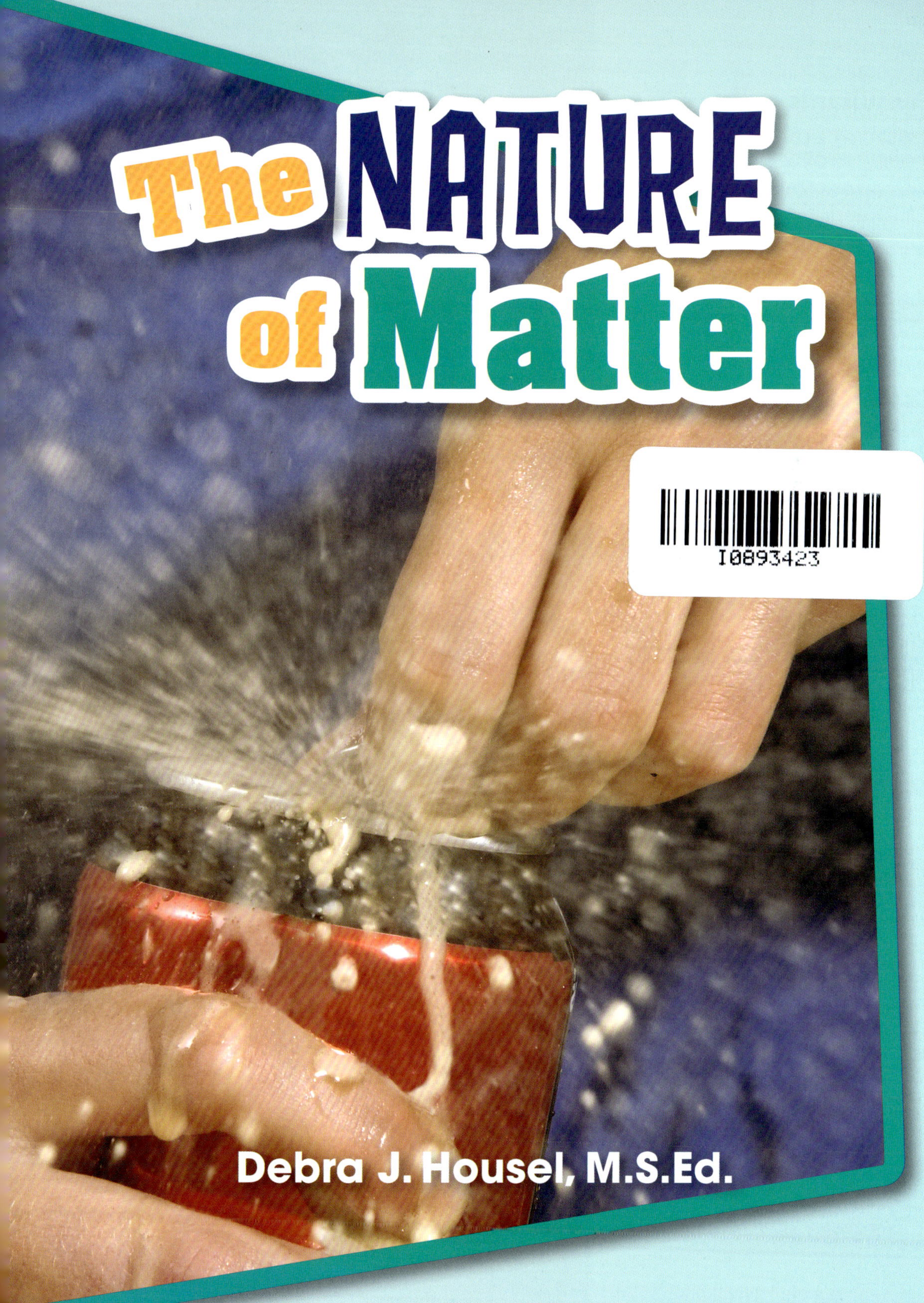

Debra J. Housel, M.S.Ed.

Consultants

Sally Creel, Ed.D.
Curriculum Consultant

Leann Iacuone, M.A.T., NBCT, ATC
Riverside Unified School District

Image Credits: Cover & p.1 Phil Degginger/Science Source; pp.28–29 (illustrations) J.J. Rudisill; all other images from Shutterstock.

Library of Congress Cataloging-in-Publication Data

Housel, Debra J., author.
The nature of matter / Debra J. Housel, M.S.Ed. ; consultant, Sally Creel, Ed.D., curriculum consultant Leann Iacuone, M.A.T., NBCT, ATC, Riverside Unified School District, Jill Tobin, California Teacher of the Year semi-finalist Burbank Unified School District.
pages cm
Summary: "Everything is made of matter! But what is matter? Anything that takes up space is matter. Matter can be a water, liquid, or gas. These are the states of matter."— Provided by publisher.
Audience: K to grade 3.
Includes index.
ISBN 978-1-4807-4603-9 (pbk.)
ISBN 978-1-4807-5070-8 (ebook)
1. Matter—Properties—Juvenile literature. I. Title.
QC173.16.H68 2015
530.4—dc23
2014014110

Teacher Created Materials
5301 Oceanus Drive
Huntington Beach, CA 92649-1030
http://www.tcmpub.com

ISBN 978-1-4807-4603-9

Table of Contents

Matter Is All Around You

Everything is made of matter. Everything! Matter can be something you see or something invisible.

You are made of matter. The air you breathe is matter. The water you drink is matter. The chair beneath you is made of matter, too.

Solids, liquids, and gases have **mass**. Mass is the amount of material in an object. They all have **volume**, too. That is the amount of space that an object takes up.

This girl is made of matter. Her pinwheels and the air that makes them spin are matter, too.

Solids Are Matter

A solid can be hard or soft. It can be big or small. Some solids are tiny. Salt, sand, and powder are tiny solids. Walls and roads are solids that are not so tiny. They are huge.

Diamond is the hardest natural material.

Carbon Is Unusual

Carbon is a solid. It can be a hard diamond or a soft pencil lead.

A solid has its own shape. If you put it into a container, it will not **conform** to the shape of the container. So if you fill a jar with plastic beads, each bead keeps its own shape.

Solids Can Change

Cutting a solid changes its size and shape. Some solids can be bent or twisted. For example, a rope is a solid. You can make it curved or straight. Clay can be made into a shape. Then, it keeps that shape until you change it again.

Play dough can be molded into many different shapes.

Solids can be joined to form a new solid. This happens when you put building blocks together to make a tower. Solids can be taken apart, too. This happens when you knock down the tower.

Wood blocks can be stacked on top of each other because they are solid.

Some Changes Cannot Be Undone

Many solids change when they are heated. If you heat a stick of butter, it will melt and become a liquid. If you heat a sheet of paper, it will burn and become ashes.

The melted butter will become solid again when it cools. It can even go back to its original shape if it cools in a mold. But the burnt paper cannot be restored. When it cools, it will still be ashes.

This liquid butter can become solid again.

Fire can appear as different colors depending on what is burning.

Paper burns and becomes ashes.

Sugar dissolves into this tea.

How Solids Behave with Liquids

Some solids **dissolve** in liquids. If you stir sugar into water, it will dissolve. It looks like the sugar is gone, but it is still there. If you taste the water, it will be sweeter than normal.

Some solids float in water. Others sink. Why? It has to do with mass. If a solid's mass pushes an equal mass of water out of the way, the thing will float. If the solid's mass pushes a smaller mass of water out of the way, it will sink.

Large chunks of ice called *icebergs* float in the ocean.

A penny sinks in water.

This lemonade takes the shape of each glass.

Liquids Are Matter

A liquid can be thick like glue, or it can be thin like juice. Either way, a liquid does not have its own shape. When a liquid is poured into a container, it takes the shape of the container. Liquid can be poured into a tall, narrow glass. It also can be poured into a short, wide glass.

When water spills, it leaves its container and spreads out.

If you spill a liquid, it spreads out. It will not stay in one shape. It does not have a consistent shape without a container.

Heating a liquid will change it. Heating water makes it boil. As water boils, it forms bubbles of water **vapor** that rise to the surface and pop. Then, the vapor rises into the air.

These bubbles are a gas that forms when water boils.

Cooling a liquid will change it, too. As water vapor in the air cools, it forms clouds. The darker the cloud, the more water vapor it holds.

If you put a glass of juice in the freezer, it will slowly become a solid. A popsicle starts out as a liquid. It cools into a solid.

The first popsicle was invented in 1905 by an 11-year-old boy named Frank Epperson.

Evaporation and Condensation

Evaporation occurs as a liquid dries up. On Monday night, it rains. You see a puddle on Tuesday. By Wednesday, the puddle is gone. Where did it go? The puddle's water became a vapor. It is in the air.

The water in this teapot is so hot that it's evaporating.

This vapor will change back into liquid water. When this happens, it is called **condensation**. The water may form dew on the grass. Dew forms when the water vapor in the air cools. If it is very cold, the dew turns into frost. Frost is frozen dew.

Condensation forms on a cold window that comes into contact with hot, humid air.

Gases Are Matter

Gas is a state of matter. Air is made of several gases. It is mostly nitrogen with some oxygen. You cannot see air, but you can feel it moving on a windy day.

Most gases cannot be seen. Yet smoke, fog, and steam are visible. Gas does not have its own shape. It spreads out to fill a space or a container. If you have an empty jar, it is actually full of air. When you blow into a balloon, the air takes the shape of the balloon.

Gas to the Rescue!

Air bags fill with gas quickly to help protect people in a car crash.

Smoke rises from this fire. It spreads out and fills the air.

It is difficult to see this mountain because it is covered in fog.

Gases Drift

Gases do not stay in one place. They drift. That is why you can smell an odor far from its source. For example, perfume is a liquid. When you open the bottle, some of it evaporates. The vapor spreads through the room. A person standing on the other side of the room will smell the perfume. Air fresheners work the same way.

Carbon Dioxide

Carbon dioxide is a gas that makes bubbles in soda.

The red arrows show warm air rising. The blue arrows show cool air sinking.

Gases Can Change

Cooling a gas can change it. Steam is water vapor. When steam cools, it becomes liquid water. If the water cools enough, it freezes and becomes ice.

Heating a gas can change it, too. Hot air rises. Cooler air rushes in to take its place. This is how your home is heated. Warm air rises from the furnace. Cooler air falls into the furnace. The air gets heated and is sent back into the house.

Heating air makes the wind blow. The sun warms the air, which rises. Cool air moves into its place. This movement makes wind blow the clouds around.

Natural Gas

Natural gas is a vapor that can dry clothes or cook food.

States of Matter

Hot noodle soup has all three kinds of matter. It has a solid, a liquid, and a gas—noodles, broth, and steam.

Water changes its state often. We notice it often in winter. Within hours, water can change from a vapor (in a cloud), to a solid (snow), and to a liquid (as it melts). But matter mostly stays in the state it is in.

That is good news. We expect milk to be liquid, chairs to be solid, and air to be gas. Think how weird it would be if a chair were a liquid or if milk were a gas!

Matter Has Properties

Tree bark is rough, hard, and brown. Those are some of its properties.

Steam is a gas.
Broth is a liquid.
Noodles are a solid.

Let's Do Science!

What states of matter can you observe? See for yourself!

What to Get

- drinking glass
- large bowl
- paper napkin
- water

What to Do

1. Fill a large bowl about two-thirds full with water.

2. Wad up the paper napkin. Press it into the bottom of the drinking glass.

3. Turn the glass upside down and press it into the bottom of the bowl.

4. Does the napkin get wet? Why or why not? What states of matter do you see in this experiment? Explain.

Glossary

condensation—the process by which a gas cools and becomes a liquid; small drops of water that form on a cold surface

conform—to take the shape or outline of something else

dissolve—to mix with a liquid and become part of the liquid

evaporation—the process of changing from a liquid to a gas

mass—the amount of matter (material) in something

mold—a container that is used to give its shape to something that is poured or pressed into it

vapor—a liquid in the form of a gas, or tiny drops of water mixed with the air

volume—the amount of space that something takes up

Index

Your Turn!

The Matter of Cocoa

What states of matter are in a steaming hot cup of cocoa with marshmallows? Draw a picture of the drink. Label each type of matter.